Pearls From My Heart

A Book of Poetry and Inspirational Writing

To Ms. Gayle King, I Pray that this book finds you well. During the Pandemic I was Inspired to write this book of Poetry. I am a Chef by trade but my heart has moved me to write. Love Shannon Morgan 5/19/21 Psalms 37:23

Shannon Morgan

S.D. MORGAN MANUSCRIPTS

Dedication

I would like to say thank you to my Lord and Savior Jesus Christ for the inspiration and the strength to write this book, "Pearls from my Heart". While writing this, I used my inner voice. Because of life's experiences, I am now doing it freely without guilt or shame through the use of pen and paper. I am not ashamed to say I love you Lord. You are my everything and I am nothing without you.

I would also like to dedicate this book to the loving memory of my mother, Glenda L. Green, and to my mother's only sister, Aunt Janie White. My mother loved to read books and write. The memory that stands out most about my mother is always seeing her with a writing pad, a pen, and of course, a book, on her coffee table. My mother and her sister were prolific women — funny, intelligent, and witty. I can only dream to be half the woman that Glenda Green and Aunt Janie were.

I cannot express how much I miss my mother so I honor her through this writing that God has enabled me to do. I pray that the reader of this book would open their hearts and mind to journey with me in my writing of poetry and inspirational stories.

I cannot forget my earthly father, Richard Green. I love you daddy. Thank you for your service. You are my hero.

These writings were produced through life's "nesses — brokenness, joyfulness, loneliness, and righteousness. God has been my "tour guide" through many mountain tops and valley's low, and I thank him for them all. Often, we look back on our past mistakes with regret. It is those mistakes that mold us, and our past failures are what gives us the strength to get up and do it again until we succeed. My God is wise and all knowing. The mistakes that I made were designed for the path that I am on today. I encourage you, reader, to love who you are and where you are today, because it is preparing you for the plan that God has for your life tomorrow.

Jeremiah 29:11 For I know the thoughts that I think toward you, saith the Lord, thought of peace, and not evil, to give you an expected end.

CONTENTS

Psalms 37:3-5

Vs. 3 Trust in the lord, and do good; so shalt thou dwell in the land, and verily thou shalt be fed

Vs. 4 delight thyself also in the lord; and he shall give thee the desires of thine heart

Vs. 5 commit your way to the Lord, trust also in him, and he will do it.

INTRODUCTION

So here I go, all nerves and butterflies, pushing them aside as I move forward with this book. After seeking God through prayer, fasting, and studying the word of God for direction and guidance, I am ready to introduce the world to "Pearls From My Heart". I cannot tell you how many times I have read my poems to my family and friends. I'm sure I got on their nerves asking for their honest feedback. If you are someone that I have read to, thank you for your patience with me, thank you for being honest with me, and most importantly, thank you for loving me. I must have written and rewritten some of these poems a dozen times…and yes, I have even completely removed some of the writings from this book because it just wasn't time. I didn't want my writing to be out of my own selfish desire, but I wanted to be able to touch someone's heart with the words from my heart.

You may find that some of the poems are a little controversial and may make some people uncomfortable, as a lot of my writing addresses the issues of racial injustice that continue to loom in our lives. I chose to write about this issue because it is so troubling, as all men were (supposedly) created equal. 2020 exposed some very ugly truths about the racial divide that so many people are unwilling to see or address. After more than 200 years of hatred and racial divide, it saddens me to say that there are times when it feels like we have not made very much progress—ten steps forward and eight steps back. We still have a long way to go, so we should not be afraid to speak out against injustice.

We all know that 2020 was a challenging year...a year of losses. Some were great losses and words cannot express the amount of grief for those who are no longer with us. 2020 has also restored, as well as torn apart families. Marriages were healed, and unfortunately, some were broken, in addition to hidden mental health issues rising to the surface. It was a year in which people perfected their talents and gifts. I have been writing for years but I never shared it with anyone for fear of rejection and the Big "J"—Judgment.

To all writers out there and even to those who are aspiring to write, hats off to you. It takes a lot of courage to write and publish your thoughts for others to read and critique.

I promised my mother eight years ago that I would write a book, but it wasn't until COVID-19 when we went into lockdown that my faith kicked in full gear. So here it is, Mom. I only wish you could be here to say that you are proud of me. God bless you all.

Habakkuk 2:2-3

Vs. 2 And the Lord answered me, and said, Write the vision and make it plain upon tables, that he may run that readeth it.

Vs. 3 For the vision is yet for an appointed time, but at the end it shall speak, and not lie: though it tarry, wait for it: because it will surely come, it will not tarry

"Skin"

I have never shared this with my family but as a young girl, and even through a better part of my adulthood, I often struggled with self-esteem. For a very long time, I felt that my hair wasn't long enough, I wasn't the right size and yes, I am ashamed to say that I even had some insecurities about my skin. This poem was written not only for me but for anyone who has struggled with their identity, skin, size, or other areas where there is a lack of self-confidence. I am here to encourage you to love who God created you to be. I want you to know that you are beautiful—light, dark, mocha, or vanilla. Love the skin in which God has placed your beautiful soul.

Never change your outer appearance to appease others. Some people may not like your skin because they are not comfortable in their skin. Love you. I have written three poems—"Skin", "Beautiful", and "This Is Me" for those who have struggled with self-confidence. Remember, God made us all in his image. What other people see is only the outer shell of you. God sees the heart of you. Beauty begins on the inside and reflects outwardly by what you say and do.

Genesis 1:27

*So, God created man in his own image.
In the image of God created he him; male and female,
he created them.*

"SKIN"

We were made from so many shades of Black, brown, and even some caramel; some have tried everything to get this skin, but this melanin is not for sale.

you can't lay in the sun, you can't spray this skin on, you're going to have to ask my creator, he chiseled this skin that I live in and all the beauty within and said daughter beware of your haters.

I made your skin and handcrafted you from your mother's womb, then I looked at the Picasso and said she may not know that she belongs in an art room.

The sun reflects its beautiful rays of the golden-brown skin that I'm in, the various hues that glistened through as if I was bathed in oil then wrapped in foil then put on display and admired by women and men.

this skin is only one layer of me you see it only goes so deep, my beauty runs for miles and miles you will get tired and want to sleep, trying to get to the end of my skin; it's for the strong and not the weak.

creams for skincare can't help you get there, neither can Botox or pills, thousands of dollars and spending long hours in a tanning bed that only kills.

so, love who you are, admire this skin from afar and acknowledge beauty when you see it, this skin has been through a lot, spit on with snot, beaten and shot, hung from a tree to rot, and still it's dumbfounded by men.

So, in conclusion, don't get a contusion trying to wrap yourself in this skin, it will always be a mystery if you research our history where we come from and where we've been.

My Life Matters

It was a challenge to write this poem, along with the other poems pertaining to the racial divide. I can't count how many times I sat on my couch in 2020 and cried as I watched another Black man murdered in public view. I cried because it could have been someone in my family—my son, grandsons, or brothers. I can't imagine the pain and grief of losing one of them simply because someone felt as if their life didn't matter. Numerous families have been left without closure, asking the loaded question, "WHY God?" Why after all of these years do we still have the same conversations around dinner tables and water coolers: "When will the killings and hatred end?" The divide is real, the hatred is real, and it is blatant and no longer kept hidden behind closed doors. I pray daily for the love of Christ to reign in our hearts. I pray for forgiveness and apologies, but the reality is that I may not get to see it in my lifetime, and I doubt that it will happen in my grandchildren's lifetime either. I'm not so sure that the marches and the protesting will change much, but I support the efforts to make our voices heard in a peaceful manner. I pray for the people whose hearts are filled with animosity towards people of color and that we would remember that in the sight of God, we all matter.

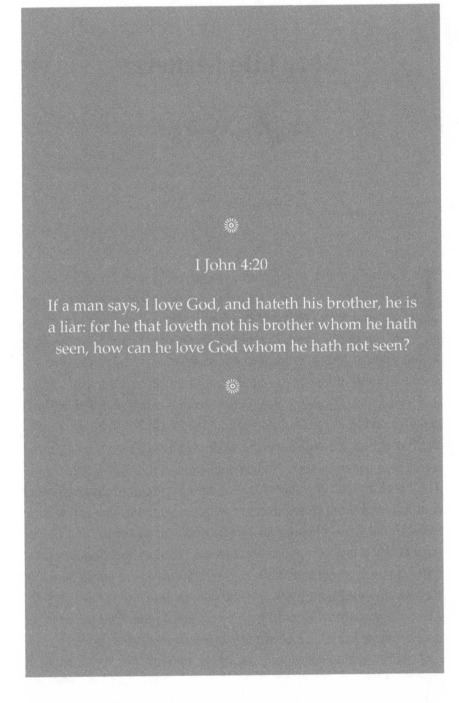

I John 4:20

If a man says, I love God, and hateth his brother, he is
a liar: for he that loveth not his brother whom he hath
seen, how can he love God whom he hath not seen?

"My Life Matters"

We raise our fist, we pump our fist, because we live in a country that is racist, what is this, stop don't resist, Black lives matter. Officer my hands are up please don't shoot what's that splatter black men are dying and their life matters.

This man had a future he was going somewhere he was a college graduate, a diploma that he worked hard to get. He worked to pay for it, wasn't slinging dope just to make it, shouting to the world finally I made it.

I'm doing good I got out the hood I have a beautiful home my floors are made of hardwood I'm doing everything that a black man should.

Raising a family, nothing was handed to me, no longer in agony from the pain of poverty, no bill collectors chasing me, did you catch that I was **debt free**.

Here you came with your guns to blow away all of my dreams, if you would have heard what I said instead you saw skin and wanted me dead, did my dark skin offend you when I asked what did I do, no you became enraged, you made a decision that erased my vision and now I'm asleep in my grave.

so yes black lives matter that's not just chatter we're dying at an alarming rate, all lives don't have to worry about being pulled over and getting shot because of hate.

your hatred is spreading like an infectious disease, the death of a black man is the only cure you see.

it's an anger and hatred that has a stench from the inside out and the smells of hell that comes out of your mouth, this is homegrown racism that is taught from the crib running down your chin like drool on a bib.

black lives matter and I will shout it from the mountaintop we will not be equal until the killing stop, until the weapons drop, until we walk hand in hand and live on the same block.

your daughters a prom Queen And my daughter is a T.H.O.T. getting the same education or maybe not?

black lives matter, my life matters, we're raising up from the ashes of this racial chatter.

We should not be afraid when we see a cop with a badge, filling up our prisons with black men and the morgues with toe tags.

so don't get mad when I march through the streets pounding my chest like the drums with a beat.

I'm black and I'm proud from the crown of my head to the soles of my feet.

you can try to silence us and say our lives don't matter with yourself righteous attitude thinking you're better, the harder you try the louder we will get, we are here to stay you can't wipe us away, lift every voice because what we have to say matters.

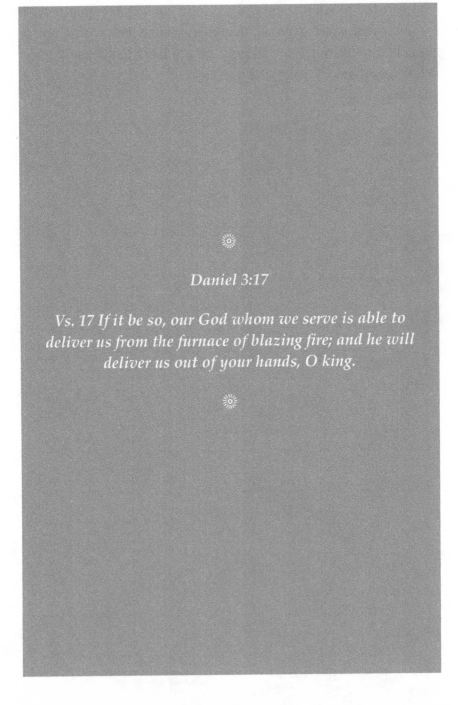

Daniel 3:17

Vs. 17 If it be so, our God whom we serve is able to deliver us from the furnace of blazing fire; and he will deliver us out of your hands, O king.

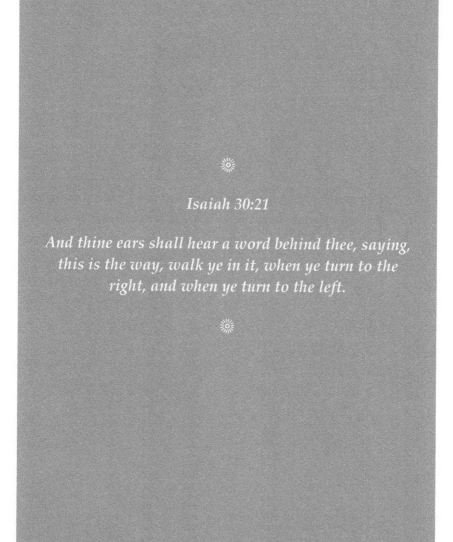

Isaiah 30:21

And thine ears shall hear a word behind thee, saying,
this is the way, walk ye in it, when ye turn to the
right, and when ye turn to the left.

"Time waits for no man"

My prayer is that as you read this poem, that we understand that it is arrogant to think that we have all the time in the world when we don't. Please pay close attention to the things going on in the world such as natural disasters, murders, hatred, and even the virus. God has given us time to get right with him and with others. Tomorrow is not promised to anyone. Please read Ecclesiastes 3:1-7. God is letting us know that there is a time for everything, but what can you do when your time is up? We have time for the internet, social media, and other things that can't save us. Please make time for God and not only when there is a need.

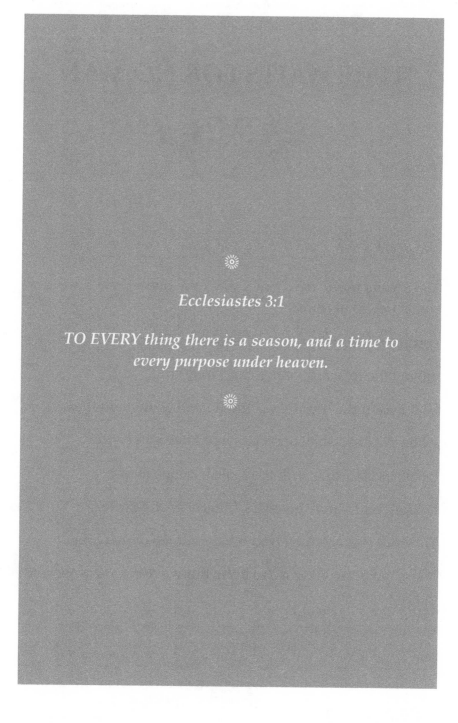

Ecclesiastes 3:1

TO EVERY thing there is a season, and a time to every purpose under heaven.

"TIME WAITS FOR NO MAN"

Time waits for no man God is the only one who holds precious time in his hand

you see he has the power to do as he will,

move time forward, or just hold time still.

God was in the beginning, and he will be there in the end,

when the Lord shall appear, every knee will bend.

Do not waste time with the foolish things in life,

holding on to unforgiveness, bitterness and strife.

Time has been an unsolved mystery to all of mankind,

We may know when we're born, but we don't know the end of time.

we rush through life wasting away each and every day,

Not slowing down to help mankind, we push the helpless out of our way

we no longer take the time to thank God for each day,

you can't rewind the hands of time when you're asleep in your grave.

We can't wait to graduate because a new life will begin,

the start of our careers and families where you're going and where you've been.

Time will wait for no man, it will move on with or without you, God has given us time, and he is watching to see what you're going to do.

Social media has found a way to consume all of our time,

Facebook wakes us up, while Twitter rocks us to sleep, we have eased God out of our lives, and we only call on him when were in need.

God has blessed us with 24 hours in a day

we give him what is left when we say I'm just too tired to pray

assuming that he will bless us to see another day

The Lord says my child, how much time will you spend with me

I don't know Lord you will just have to **Wait** and see

I'm sure I have plenty of time before you come to get me.

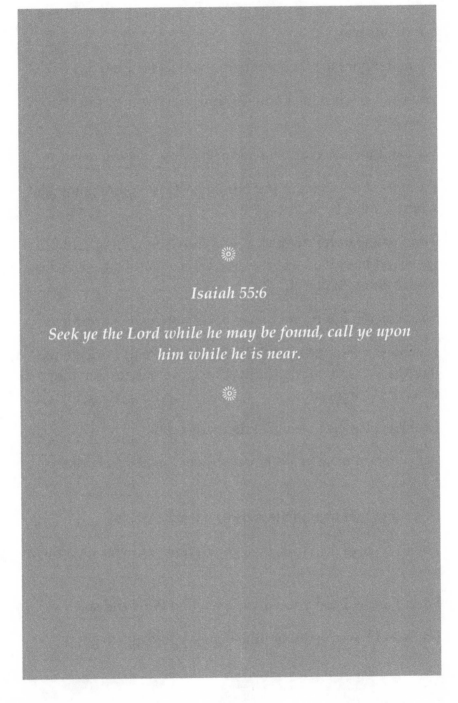

Isaiah 55:6

Seek ye the Lord while he may be found, call ye upon him while he is near.

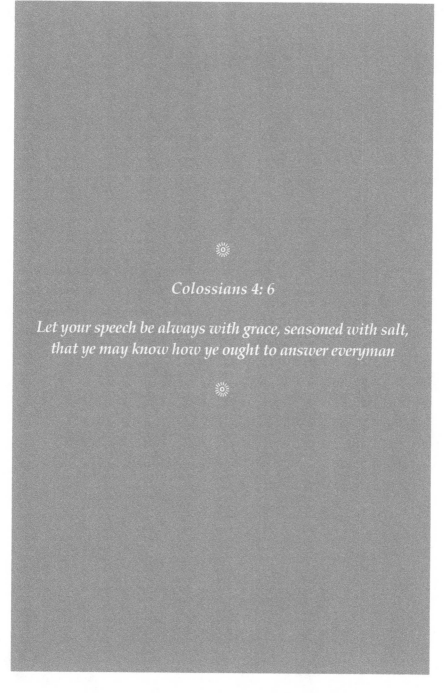

Colossians 4: 6

Let your speech be always with grace, seasoned with salt,
that ye may know how ye ought to answer everyman

"Beautiful"

Dear Lord, this was written for my beautiful daughter, as well as my daughter-in-law, and for all of the women out there who sometimes feel defeated, overwhelmed, and unappreciated. I pray that you know that your hard work and perseverance does not go unnoticed. May you keep your head up, stay focused, and believe that it will all pay off in the end. I have been there myself, dear Lord, and it was only because of the grace of God (my foundation), prayer, family, and friends that I was able to make it through the hard times. My prayer is that you stay strong my beautiful daughters and trust in the Lord Always.

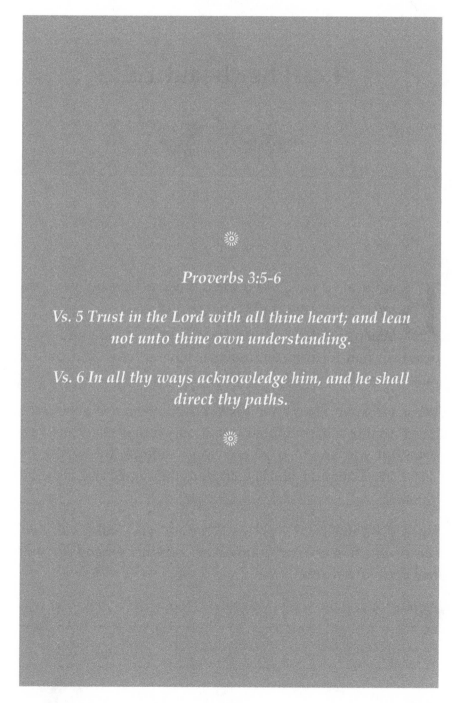

✺

Proverbs 3:5-6

Vs. 5 Trust in the Lord with all thine heart; and lean not unto thine own understanding.

Vs. 6 In all thy ways acknowledge him, and he shall direct thy paths.

✺

"I call her beautiful"

B eautiful you are, I know this much is true, because you are a part of me, and I am a part of you.

When you smile it reflects the love of God and your beautiful nature from within, you have a glow that only a mother would know it goes deeper than your skin.

When I hear you laughing it is like smooth jazz to my ears, it has a rhythm a harmonic beat that only a musician can hear. Beautiful you are, God placed you inside of my womb, he said to me daughter, she is your daughter, nurture her as she blooms.

He said when she cries you will cry and you will not understand why, that is when you will be one with her and she will feel your love inside.

Beautiful you are when you hurt I, too, will be in pain, I will be there to hold your crown, when you want to bow your head in shame.

That's right you are a queen and on a pedestal is where you belong, I gave you a biblical name so you would know that your roots run deep and strong.

Beautiful, I know there are times when you feel like the weight of the world is on your back, that is God making you stronger and keeping you on track.

You are beautiful and you should never allow anything to define who you are, nothing can ever pull you down, because you are among the stars.

If someone tries to tear you down, it's because they need to build themselves up, they are inferior to someone superior and they know they will never measure up.

Beautiful, you are a mother who has to wear many crowns, a woman's work is never done even after she lay down. I see you even when the stress is more than you can bare, know that I am here for you and your burdens I will share.

Whatever you're going through in this life, don't ever throw in the towel, you don't need to see God to know what he is doing, just push through every mile,

I need you to know that I call you beautiful and I'm proud to call you my child.

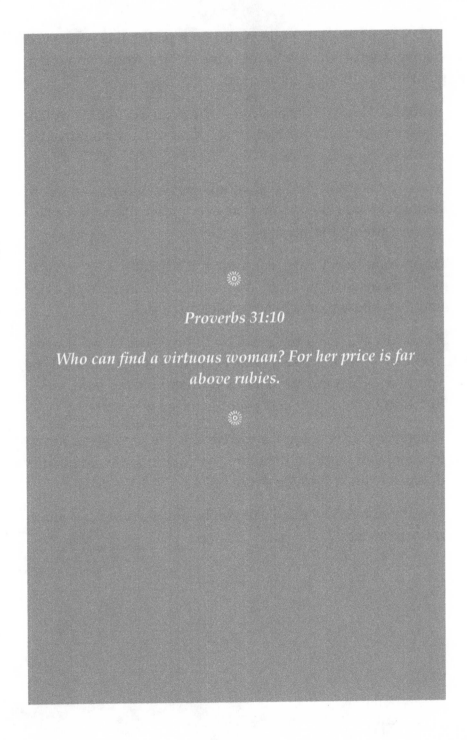

Proverbs 31:10

Who can find a virtuous woman? For her price is far above rubies.

"Crown of glory"

This poem was written for my beloved mother, Glenda L. Green. I was honored to call her Mom. God chose a courageous woman to mother eight beautiful children.

Dear Lord, you are all wise and all knowing. You know how much I miss my mother, but your will is so perfect. You delivered mom from suffering in this life so that she could rest with you in eternal glory. What a beautiful example of strength and resilience she showed us during her short battle with Lung Cancer.

When she transitioned from this life on April 12, 2013, she was 74 years old. Words cannot express how broken I was when we lost her. It was hard for me to imagine my world and my life without my mom-- without her wisdom, intelligence, guidance, and love.

Crown of Glory was befitting for mom because she loved her Sunday hats, and she would rock them with so much class. God traded her Sunday morning "crowns" for an everlasting Crown of Glory, and I know that I will see her again someday.

II Corinthians 5:1

*For we know that if our earthly house of this
tabernacle were dissolved, we have a building of God,
a house not made with hands, eternal in the heavens.*

"CROWN OF GLORY"

I am a child of God, no longer with human eyes can I be seen,

I'm wearing my crown of glory,

I'm resting in the arms of my king

I know that you will miss me,

The way we use to laugh and share our stories,

It's ok if you want to cry, but remember I have my crown of glory

You see pain no longer knows my address,

I am free from heartache and despair,

I traded my beautiful Sunday morning hats,

For the crown that I now wear.

With the help of God, I raised each of my children,

I gave each one of them a special part of me,

So, children lift your head and wipe your eyes and know that I am now free.

I am a child of God and I was woven with love and pride,

You couldn't see my crown before that's because I wore my crown inside.

I leave with all of you, memories, you have photos to reflect on my life,

I cannot wait to see you all again when you receive your Crown of Life.

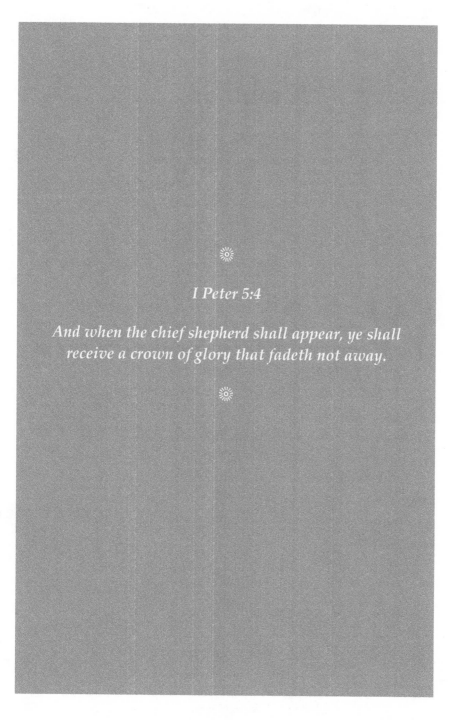

I Peter 5:4

And when the chief shepherd shall appear, ye shall receive a crown of glory that fadeth not away.

"We can't breathe"

What can I say about 2020? This was a year of exposure, brokenness, and so much pain. After many marches and protests across the United States following the death of George Floyd and other black men and women, we are far from healing. "I can't breathe." We will never forget those chilling last words spoken by George Floyd and now the chant of millions of African Americans in protest of the gross injustices of racial divide. I believe that this poem speaks volumes of how far we still have to go. I pray for healing and peace in the land. I just don't believe that it will happen in my lifetime. May this poem open up candid conversations pertaining to the ugliness of racism so that we can begin to reach across the aisle for reconciliation.

Galatians 6:9-10

Vs. 9 And let us not be weary in well doing: for in due season we shall reap, if we faint not.

Vs. 10 As we have therefore opportunity, let us do good unto all men, especially unto them who are of the household of faith.

"WE CAN'T BREATHE"

We are down on our knees, please, please, we cannot breathe. This is the situation we have been facing, segregation, desperation, so much hatred in our nation. Reformation, emancipation, mass incarceration, which is that state of being confined just like a plantation.

We can't breathe black lives are taken, in 2020 were pushing voter's registration, lack of education, manifestation; help us please we can't breathe we have faced so much rejection, lack of protection, Biden was up for the Presidential Election while Donald Trump is spreading lies like an infection. As we fight for our rights, your knee is on neck as we are losing our life, were fighting for air and our eyes are losing sight.

As our hearts beat, we march the streets, rejecting defeat, law enforcement mace us to make us weak, we can't breathe but we will not die, we will fight for our life and pray for a piece of the pie. United States of what, you mean divided and hate all of us. You shoot a black man because he went for a jog, minding his business not bothering y'all, modern day lynching is what the world saw, another black man dies without a cause.

We will never forget George Floyd's now haunting words "I can't breathe" his murder on the streets is what the world got to see. So many people said systematic racism doesn't exist, asking the question, why are they protesting and pumping their fist, what is this? We can't breathe because this country has its knees in our neck, choking out our vision to be treated equally and shown some dignity and respect.

Coronavirus is killing us, racism is dealing us a hand that belittles us, the president isn't feeling us, the police is killing us, we don't know who we can trust, in fifty years we moved from the back of the bus, sometimes our worst enemy is us, people are saying 2020 is a bust, God please we can't breathe we need you to help us.

We will stand, hand in hand, creating a chain across this land, we will be unbreakable we will let the world know, we will never give up hope, we will fight until we can't fight no more, 2020 has opened the door and exposed a sore of injustice that we will not tolerate anymore.

Isaiah 12:2

Behold, God is my salvation; I will trust and not be afraid: for the lord Jehovah is my strength and my song; he also has become my salvation.

"THIS IS ME"

I have finally accepted me, for who I am,
not who I was trying to be.

No longer am I living for others to see,

I'm walking in the freedom of just being me.

Self-love is number one not two nor three,

No, I will not love you before I first love me.

Self-love is self-care and now I'm aware,

my eyes have been opened to the facade I would wear.

My head is held high, and my shoulders are back,

I have finally accepted me, and I am staying on track.

I must admit I struggled with accepting who God created me
to be,

rejecting myself means rejecting the one who created me.

No longer comparing myself to how the world says I should look,

Long hair, a tiny waist,

fine clothes with Gucci on my pocketbook.

Self-love and acceptance is how I choose to live my life,

the only one I'm aiming to please is my Savior Jesus Christ.

This is me you can take it or leave it,

I no longer care,

Watch me walk with my short natural hair,

My confidence is from within, and you're not welcomed in there.

This Is Me, Flawless and free…

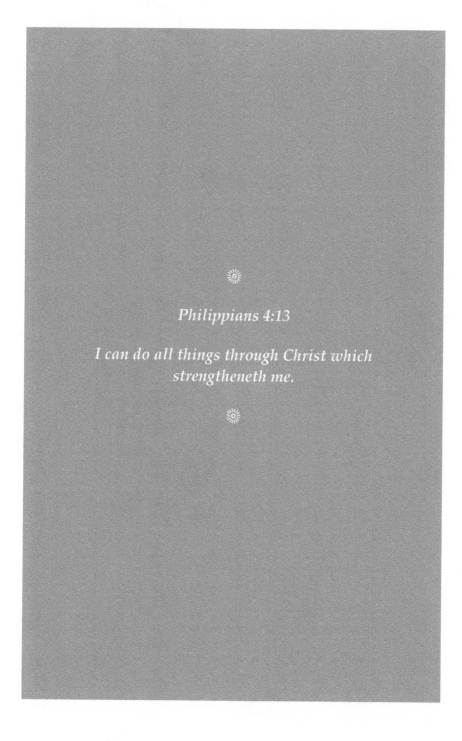

Philippians 4:13

*I can do all things through Christ which
strengtheneth me.*

Know Jesus, Know Joy

No Jesus, No joy

J Jesus

O on the inside of

Y you

"What divides you and me"

We have been divided for centuries and the more that we try to overcome that which divides, we seem to fall further back.

The bandage has been pulled back and the ugly wounds of racism have been exposed over the past four years. 2020 had exposed the deep wound of injustice, hatred, and bigotry.

The deaths of Ahmaud Arbery in February, Breonna Taylor in March, George Floyd in May, Casey Goodson and Andre Hill in December; those names were added to a long list of names of men and women who were murdered because of the line that divides us.

It seems like no one is held accountable and no laws or justice system will hold them accountable for their murderous rampage on the black community.

Dear Lord, the scale of justice continues to be unbalanced compared to other ethnicities. For we know that the stench of racial injustice fills the air, and our judicial system covers their noses and acts like nothing is wrong.

May we continue to fight for injustice and against the racial divide in our communities, workplaces, schools, and government so that our children and grandchildren can grow up and live a full and prosperous life and have a story to tell their children. We shall overcome someday with your help Lord.

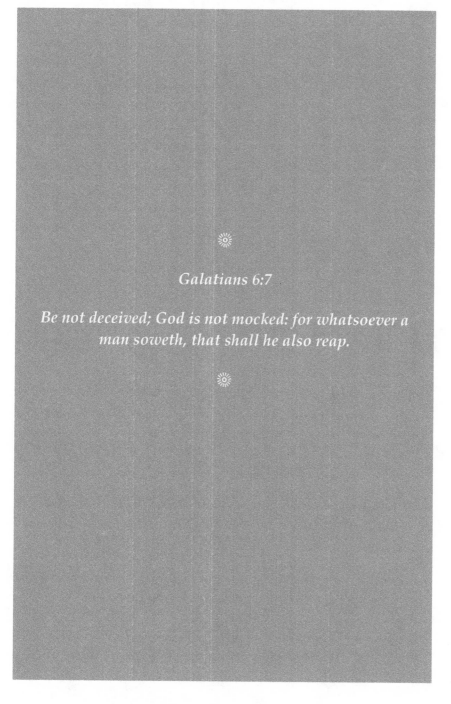

Galatians 6:7

Be not deceived; God is not mocked: for whatsoever a man soweth, that shall he also reap.

WHAT DIVIDES YOU AND ME"

The line is divided, and we stand face to face, there's an invisible line that divides you and me because of our ethnicity, yes our race

I'm sorry did I say that we are divided because of race, what I really meant to say was we are divided because of hate.

Your shield, your gun, your armor, and mace, will not cross the line so that the past can be erased.

Medgar Evers, Dr. King, and Emmett Till, their names are on a long list of black Kings and Queens that cowards have killed.

If I had a choice of what color I could be, I would choose the color of love now that is a color we all should see.

But for some reason black is the color that represents hate, you use my race to measure my success, and determine my fate.

Who gave you the authority to hate my creator, He meticulously smoothed out the color of my flesh, yet some are intimidated and only see my skin as a threat?

Dream, legacy, equality, free, these were words of hope spoken by Dr. King,

being black in America is not always what it seems, never waking up from the racial injustice dream.

For us to cross the line of divide, America must first be willing to swallow its pride,

swallow the wrong that it has believed was right,

raping and robbing us and hanging us at night,

from the weeping willows and Old Oak trees trying to eradicate the black race from being what God intended for us to be.

trying to erase our ancestry, before we were slaves living in our own country before the diseases of the infested slave ship before the waters became our grave pits.

The line of divide started oversees, you kidnapped us and now you have the nerve to hate me, because I was originated from my land of the brave

and the home where my people were free

Now that is the invisible line that has divided you and me.

Psalms 37:1-2

Vs. 1 Fret not thyself because of evildoers, neither be thou envious against the workers of iniquity

Vs. 2 for they shall soon be cut down like the grass, and wither as the green herb.

A cup filled with bitterness is a cup that has been broken inside, don't try to drink what's in someone else cup swallow your own pride.

"The time has come"

This is a day that shall go down in history-- January 20, 2021. It is the day that Senator Kamala Harris was sworn in to the second highest office in the land—Vice President of the United States of America. I am only sad that my mother and my Aunt Janie, who were historians, did not live long enough to witness this day. I believe that on that special day, women of all nationalities felt liberated, like there is nothing that we cannot do, and no office that is unreachable. The time has come for women to become equals in the workplace, in the boardrooms, in government offices, and maybe someday, the President of the United States of America. President Obama paved the way for African Americans, so now I know that anything is possible if you believe.

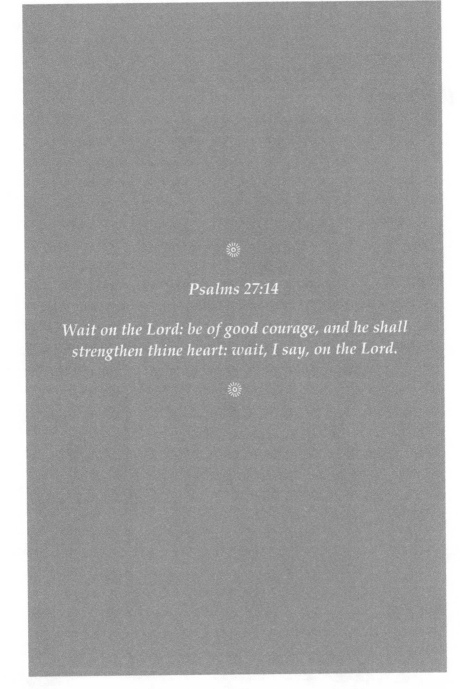

Psalms 27:14

Wait on the Lord: be of good courage, and he shall strengthen thine heart: wait, I say, on the Lord.

"THE TIME HAS COME"

Wrap your mind around this is, that is if you can,
A woman of color holding one of the highest offices in the land.

Vice President of The United States, that is a sound that will always resonate.

black women have been held back for many centuries, treated like second class citizens scrubbing floors of America on our hands and knees.

Now rise and show Madam Vice President Kamala Harris the respect she deserves,

as she walks through the White House with confidence without uttering a single word.

This woman is a trailblazer, and she is making a path for others to follow, young girls all around the world can no longer say I wish,

but can now say "I KNOW".

We are confident,

Beautiful and successful in every way,

we hold down our household and our careers and still take time to pray.

Satan get behind thee, your time is coming to an end, we no longer believe your lies and hell is your den.

Women have fought for hundreds of years just to be treat equal to men

Our time has come, and this is History in the making,

so, get out your brooms America get to sweeping up all the glass from the ceilings that women are breaking.

Isaiah 40:31

But they that wait upon the Lord shall renew their strength; they shall mount up with wings as eagles; they shall run, and not be weary; and they shall walk, and not faint.

A Crown fitted with Gold, Jasper, & Sapphire

T his was written for my three children. If you are a parent, I pray that you will appreciate the words of the poem. I know that you will understand that no two children are the same and you will certainly understand that no one has perfect children. We as parents will put our all into our children the same way God, our Father, gave his all for us. Our children will make mistakes, as we did as children and we still do as adults. Treat your children like the precious gems that they are, no matter what. God is the best example of unconditional love. He has shown us how to love and more importantly, how to forgive. I have made many mistakes as a parent, and now that my children are parents, they too will make mistakes. The important thing about making mistakes as a parent is to be ready to admit, pray, then heal from your mistakes. I was a young mother, so I had to grow up really fast, while stumbling along the way. I now know that God was the one picking me up each time I stumbled as a young mother.

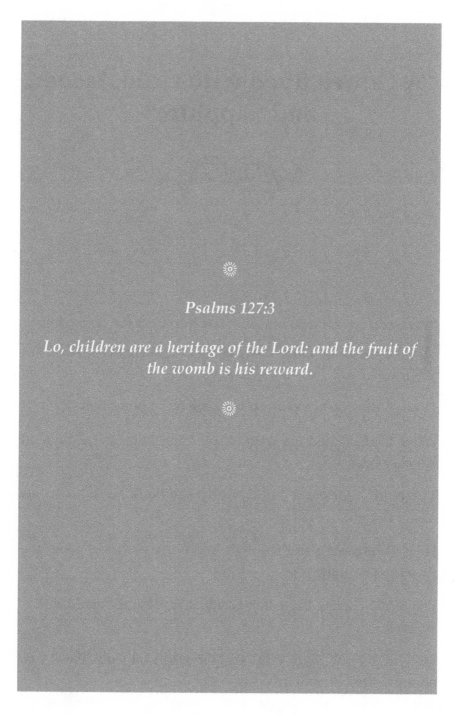

Psalms 127:3

Lo, children are a heritage of the Lord: and the fruit of the womb is his reward.

"A Crown fitted with Gold, Jasper, and Sapphire"

I wear a crown with three jewels that God fitted inside,
I call them the fruit of my womb; they are my joy and my pride.

Though they be not perfect, they are mine nonetheless,

When God blessed me with these three children, he gave me his very best.

Tyree, my oldest I would have to say he is my warrior not afraid to fight,

He is a watchman on the tower, keeping watch while his family sleeps at night.

For him I choose the color **Gold,** it represents triumph and success,

He will give his family his all and when he feels like it isn't enough, then he will give his best.

Trey, my second born king, a gentle quiet spirit, you see his fight is hidden inside,

He is protective of his heart, yet his love is his pride.

For him I choose **Jasper,** because it symbolizes strength and honesty,

He will make sure that he is always available when his loved ones are in need.

Sara, now she is the queen of my heart, she is beauty in a crowded room,

Yet her confidence sets her apart.

I choose for her **Sapphire,** a guardian of innocence and a bestower of truth,

But when her back is up against the wall, she knows exactly what to do.

Together these three complete me and to each I give a special kind of love,

I cannot handle each jewel the same, I must seek instructions from above.

I make sure that my Gold, my Jasper, and that my Sapphire are all polished with special care,

Then I carefully place them back in my crown because I know that they will be safe in there.

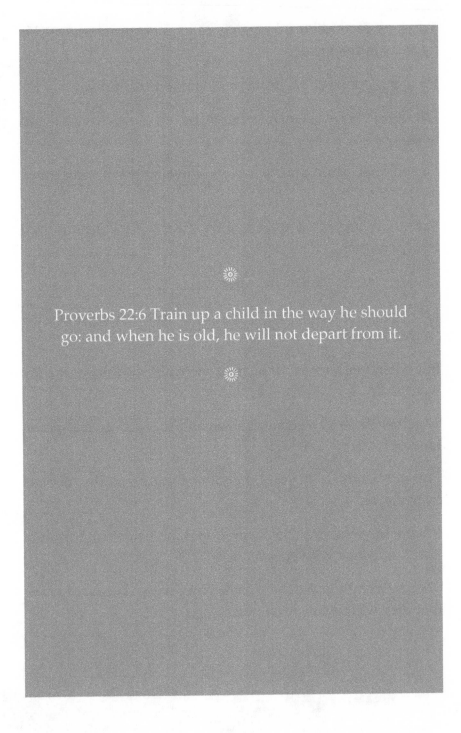

Proverbs 22:6 Train up a child in the way he should go: and when he is old, he will not depart from it.

"Black man"

This one right here can hit in so many ways. I know and have in my life, plenty of strong black men/Kings including my sons, grandsons, and my brothers. I love my black men and there are plenty of good black men out there. I just need for some of them to wake up and realize how beautiful and gifted they are and that there is a king and greatness that is waiting on the inside. Society has beaten them down for centuries—mentally, physically, and spiritually. It is time to kneel down and lift them up.

Genesis 2:7

And the Lord God formed man of the dust of the
ground and breathed into his nostrils the breath of
life; and man became a living soul.

"BLACK MAN"

Dear black man, we need for you to be strong black man,

Stop being a slave to a lifestyle that is wrong black man.

Be a leader in your homes black man,

In your community and in the church black man,

Graduate from college and be the first black man,

To break the generational curse of our black men.

Your ancestors died so that you could be free black man,

But you find pleasure in being a slave to the streets black man.

You're doing the work of the enemy black man,

He is laughing and saying I got you under my knees black man,

Your grandmother's prayers mean nothing to me black man,

Thank you for killing your own for Me black man,

You have made my job so easy black man.

Your sons and daughters will never grow up to see black man,

their father being a free black man,

Until this world gets on its knees black man,

And pray that the stronghold be released black man,

And restore the kings of our ancestry black man,

You will only pass down a generation of Weak black men.

Fight for your life in every State black man,

There is greatness that awaits our beautiful black men,

Protect the heritage of your race black man,

Don't wait for someone else to make you great black man,

Rise up and take your rightful place black man.

✺

Isaiah 43:7

Even every one that is called by my name: for I have created him for my glory, I have formed him: yea, I have made him.

Never try to measure up to who someone else want you to be, how would they measure up if they used the eyes of God to see?

✺

"A Precious PEARL"

When I prayed about the title of this book, I went to the internet to research how pearls are formed. I was blessed and surprised to discover that pearls are the only piece of jewelry that comes from a living organism. Pearls are formed from oysters, mussels, and clams.

According to **pearls.com**, "**Natural pearls form when an irritant-usually a parasite and not the proverbial grain of sand works its way into an oyster, mussel or clam. As a defense mechanism, a fluid is used to coat the irritant. Layer upon layer of this coating, called nacre; is deposited until a lustrous pearl is formed.**"

Imagine that a beautiful piece of jewelry, loved by humans and adorned on fine clothing, was manifested from a parasite called Nacre. An authentic, single pearl takes at least 3 years to form while the oyster, mussel, and clam mature. Sometimes we have to stay in a storm for a while until we mature so that God can form a pearl. When you think about life, life can produce all kinds of nacre (parasites) but when you remain focused, prayerful, and persistent, you *will find that it was worth the wait. I thank God for everything that I experienced in life that didn't kill me, but that produced a beautiful pearl. So often we do not know what God is doing, but "we know that all things work together for good to them that love God, to them who are called, according to his purpose." Romans 8:28. We are all precious in the sight of the Lord and we must remember that tests and trials come to make us strong. A real pearl is strong and cannot be broken. The only way to determine if a pearl is real is by rubbing it on your teeth. If it is gritty like sand, then it is the real deal. Just because some things are smooth, does not meant that they are real.*

"PEARLS FROM MY HEART"

If you should stumble upon
a pearl, cherish it
because it came from
my heart,
Through many tears of life's
tests and trials
the Nacre made it hard,
While the hands of Jesus Christ kept this
Precious jewel hidden, safe, and warm,
The Nacre transformed the pain of this
 life and there a single Pearl was formed,
Just at the right season this precious
Pearl was carefully removed,
This Pearl was made with
The hands of the Lord
And there my heart
Was renewed

Matthew 13:45-46

Vs. 45 Again, the kingdom of heaven is like unto a merchant man, seeking goodly pearls:

Vs. 46 Who, when he had found one pearl of great price, went and sold all that he had, and bought it.

Forgiveness is for you and forgiveness is for me, when you refuse to forgive someone who has wronged you think about who forgave your sins when he was crucified on the tree.

"Our future Generation"

There is a storm on the horizon, this is a storm unlike any that we have ever seen,

This storm is wiping out a whole generation of young adults and teens

The storm is very destructive, and it is trying to destroy our young people dreams

These youths no longer care about running for prom Kings and Queens

Marching in the bands, honor roll, or colleges to pursue great things

Playing in the halls with their friends attending all the sports games

These teens are killing teens and instead walking away from confrontation

They would rather use guns to destroy their own generation

They have no problems committing crimes because there is no recourse

They are stealing cars and robbing the elderly without any remorse

They have no fear of their parents, the police or the judicial courts

These youths aren't being raised

they are surviving the best way they know how

The streets are their home, and the grave is where they lay down

They refuse to work an honest paying job

They don't care who they rob

No one is teaching them about fear or reverence for the living God

They lack education because they have no respect for the educator

Yet they show lies, anger, malice and disrespect favor

They despise wisdom, knowledge compassion and truth

Somebody please tell me who is raising our youths

I don't know about you, but I am tired of seeing our youths on the news dying every night

Parents why are you silent these are your children stand up and fight

The enemy isn't playing he is taking them out left and right

Before they have the chance to give their life to Christ

Parents you can't "kick-it" with your children and think that it is alright

They need to see you as a role model in their life

Not all parents are at fault, I get that too

Some children choose to hang- out with the wrong group

Children don't you know that Your body and drugs are not for sale

Parents get your children and pull them out of the gates of hell

We need you alive so that you will have a story to tell.

This is not the same storm such as a natural disaster

This storm isn't slowing down it's moving faster

It's taking the lives of our future generation

Parents if you don't wake up

Funeral plan is the only thing that we will be making

Ephesians 6:1-4

Vs. 1 Children obey your parents in the Lord: for this is right.

Vs. 2 Honor thy father and mother; (which is the first commandment with promise)

Vs. 3 That it may be well with thee, and thou mayest live long on the earth

Vs. 4 And ye fathers, provoke not your children to wrath: but bring them up in the nurture and admonition of the Lord.

Don't be afraid to reach down and give your fellowman a helping hand,

You may be the strength that they need when their legs are too weak to stand.

"THIS HOUSE"

Dear Lord, this house was built with many tools used by man's hands,

The foundation and the walls were erected

so that when the storms would come it would stand.

But inside these walls there are special tools,

That you can only get from God above,

They are hammered with faith,

nailed in honesty,

and sealed with prayers and love,

Now with these special tools

this house is guaranteed to stand,

Because with the strong foundation from God

It is built on a solid rock and not sinking sand.

Matthew 7:24-25

Vs. 24 Therefore whosoever heareth these sayings of mine and doeth them, I will liken him unto a wise man, which built his house upon a rock:

Vs. 25 And the rain descended, and the floods came, and the winds blew, and beat upon that house; and it fell not: for it was founded upon a rock.

"You are not your pain"

Pain is not something that anyone is looking forward to or misses when it's gone, but pain comes in many forms and for many reasons. Pain can come in the form of grief due to the loss of a loved one or even a breakup. Pain can also be in the physical body. No matter how it enters your life, we do our best to endure until it is gone. I have had to endure pain, and when I look back, I know beyond a shadow of a doubt that I was never alone. There was a comforter with me, and he saw me through it all. Pain is only for a season and Jesus has given us his word that he will help us no matter what that pain may be, so do not become one with your pain. I pray that you will be at peace and receive your healing. May you find comfort in these words.

❋

Revelations 21:4

And God shall wipe away all tears from their eyes;
and there shall be no more death, neither sorrow, nor
crying, neither shall there be any more pain: for the
former things are passed away.

❋

"YOU ARE NOT YOUR PAIN"

I see the pain that you wear on your face,
The pain of your past that you have tried to escape.

Your pain has hindered you from doing all the things that you use to do,

Your pain is like a puppet and it controls you.

Pain is your name you have been one for far too long,

You're afraid to walk away and pain is your song

You were not made to live your life this way,

Telling your pain "It's ok you can stay"

Pain is not meant to be a permanent resident,

 living inside of you without paying any rent.

A life of poverty can bring with it pain,

Struggling to make ends meet

So, if you are bound to a life without change

Pain can be an abusive relationship,

Instead of aborting,

you go down with the ship.

Some associate pain with a life of racial divide,

 the pain of fighting for equality yet always denied.

 Physical mental and emotional pain

Jesus is a healer just call on his name

 Release all of your pain and release it by faith

 he will comfort and heal you in exchange for his Grace.

You are no longer known by your pain

 God has delivered you and given you a new name

Psalms 34:18-19

Vs. 18 The Lord is near to the brokenhearted and saves those who are crushed in spirit.

Vs. 19 Many are the afflictions of the righteous: but the Lord delivers him out of them all.

If you only had one day to love, who would you choose?

Act like everyday is your last day to love, even if it is someone who doesn't love you.

"Sisters"

Dear Lord, this poem is to all of my sisters-- black, white, Hispanic, Asian, or whatever your nationality may be. More importantly, this is to my black sisters. For centuries we have looked down, stepped over, disrespected, and talked about one another as if the world has not already done that enough. Father, I will admit that even I have been guilty of these unrighteous fruits (and this is me being real with me). Thank you God for revealing to me that <u>ALL</u> women are beautiful. What would it look like if we supported one another, encouraged one another, and put someone else before ourselves? We would look more like you. I love my Sisters and if I have ever hurt anyone with the words from my mouth or by my actions, I am truly sorry.

My mother had a very close friend who was her best friend for 50 years, until the day my mother died. Ms. Barbara Taylor and Glenda Green did not always agree with one another and they were not perfect, but they were the epitome of "Sisters". To this day when I talk to Ms. Taylor, she still cries and talks about how much she misses my mom. Friend is a word that has been misused and misunderstood. I think of these two women that endured so many tests and trials in their 50 years of friendship, yet they remained unbreakable until then end.

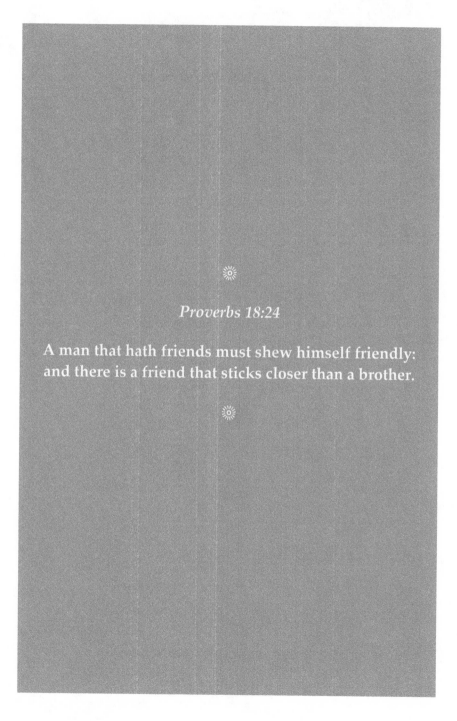

Proverbs 18:24

A man that hath friends must shew himself friendly:
and there is a friend that sticks closer than a brother.

"SISTERS"

Let me help you up my sister,
When it feels like Life has knocked you down,

I choose to be that sister, the one who will

Hold you up when no one else is around.

I promise not to use my words as a weapon,

To kill your Spirit deep inside,

I promise to be that sister that will get on her knees,

and pray for you when you cry.

I will be your biggest cheerleader

When it feels like your dreams are about to die,

I will be the one to remind you

That You can do all things through Christ Jesus,

because the Spirit of God lives inside.

My sister, I will be the one to listen and laugh with you

When the hours on the clock tick away

And when your heart has been broken

I will provide a shoulder for your head to lay

When you want to dance my sister,

I will dance with you, even if it's in the rain,

I will speak healing words when your joy has turned to pain.

When you are barely making ends meet

To six figures in your bank account,

My love and loyalty to my sisters has no dollar amount.

You are me and I am you, and we may not always agree

But I promise you that I will be your pillar of strength,

That's Because I know that you will be the same for me.

We may not share the same DNA, but you are my "Sister"

And I thank God for you every time I pray.

John 4:7

Beloved, let us love one another: for love is of God; and every one that loveth is born of God, and knoweth God.

Rejection is a hard pill to swallow especially when you have done all you can do

Treat others with kindness because that pill goes down different when it is given back to you.

Humans Dehumanized

This poem speaks for itself, with regard to the inhumane treatment and cruelty that our ancestors had to endure at the hands of their taskmasters. All they had were their spiritual songs and their faith in God for strength.

Genesis 3:7

And the lord said, I have surely seen the affliction of my people which are in Egypt and have heard their cry by reason of their taskmaster; for I know their sorrow.

"Humans Dehumanized"

I can hear their voices crying out from the graves,
I can smell the blood of my ancestors who were slaves,

They were not considered humans more like property,

They were on a stage, put on display for all the buyers to see,

I am in their DNA and their DNA lives in me,

I am the voice of my brothers and sister, that died as slaves before me.

Our women would give birth and before they could nurse

their babies were ripped from their breast,

these women were put right back out in the fields

with no time to heal or rest.

Our black men were beaten, they were beaten down

In their mind, body and souls,

They would pray and beg God for death because it was the only freedom

That they would know.

Their tears were their pillows,

And pain would wrap around them like sheets,

They would wear calluses as hands and blood was like shoes on their feet.

The cotton fields became their graveyards and sorrow is what they would eat.

Before they would rise to see another day,

They were already covered in defeat.

Hope was hopeless,

And joy they never knew, they could not read or write,

their day would begin in the cotton fields before

The sun cracked the sky with daylight.

Weekends were no exception and holidays well that was just another day,

from the crib to the grave, they tried to be brave

they were Humans dehumanized this was the life of a slave.

✺

In this life you will experience some hard times, go through it with grace,

It is those hard times that build your spiritual muscles while you walk by faith.

✺

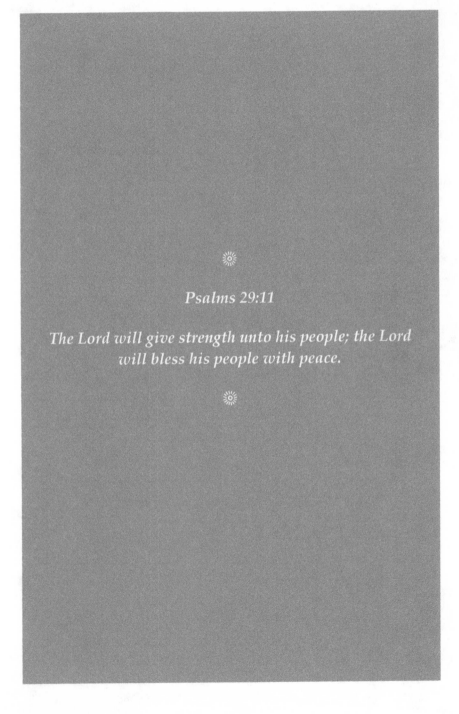

Psalms 29:11

The Lord will give strength unto his people; the Lord will bless his people with peace.

PEACE FOR YOUR PIECES

Peace for your pieces is very near and dear to my heart because I truly understand what it means to be broken and to find Peace in my Savior. I pray that before you read this particular poem, you would take a moment to reflect in your heart, a time when you were broken, and it was nothing but the Peace of God that restored you. If you have not experienced the Peace of God, I encourage you to get alone with God and invite him into your heart. Believe me, he will do it for you. Please don't search for Peace in a relationship, job, family, or material things. You will never find it there. It's inside of you. Just ask God to take you there.

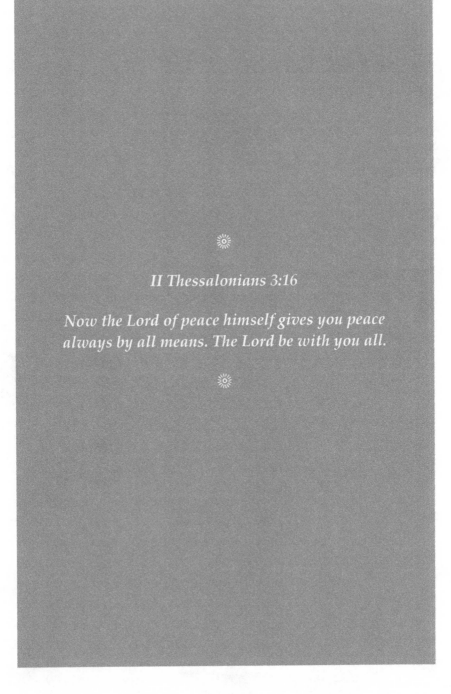

II Thessalonians 3:16

Now the Lord of peace himself gives you peace always by all means. The Lord be with you all.

PEACE FOR YOUR PIECES

If you don't know peace, I have something to share with you

Peace held me together better than anyone else could ever do

I never knew that I could feel such a calming precious Peace

But I had to go through some tests and trials and release some things in me

Peace is what comforts you in the middle of a long night

When your tears soak your pillow but somehow you know it's going to be alright

Peace will hold you together while mending all of your broken pieces

Peace is when the Lord says let go, it's ok to release it

"IT" can be anything from sickness to a broken relationship

Maybe it's a wayward child that you have tried over and over to fix

Peace is harmless in fact it will give you a renewed life

Peace says this battle is not yours, but it is mine to fight

Peace is like standing in the midst of a fire without being consumed

Peace is knowing you're not in the fire alone because Jesus is the room

When you have Peace, you can walk away from a good paying job

Peace is when you come out unharmed after being robbed

You have Peace when the doctor says there is nothing else we can do

Peace whispers in your ears I have already Healed You

He will exchange your pieces for His loving Peace

His Peace is like giving sight to the blind and beauty is all you see

You can try to find Peace in cars, commodities and clothes

But none of those things can ever fill the broken pieces of your soul

Peace is priceless you see there is no dollar amount

Peace is like being a millionaire without a single dollar in your bank account

Peace is knowing that Jesus is someone you simply can't live without

John 14:27

Peace I leave with you, my Peace I give unto you: not as the world giveth, give I unto you. Let not your heart be troubled, neither let it be afraid.

John 16:33

These things I have spoken to you, so that in Me you may have a peace. In the world you have tribulations, but take courage; I have overcome the world

Isaiah 26:3 Thou wilt keep him in perfect peace, whose mind is stayed on thee: because he trusts in thee.

You are Unbreakable

In my lifetime I have had the pleasure of meeting some of the most resilient people. They have truly withstood the many challenges of life and still managed to be unbreakable. I know that my inner strength comes from the Lord, something that I am truly proud to say. I don't have the time to discuss all that God has done for me, but I am here to tell you that I am Unbreakable.

This was written for someone who may feel like they can't take life anymore or they're ready to throw in the towel. Well, I am here to throw the towel back at you because you are Unbreakable. Remember, tests and trials come to make you strong…and you are stronger than you realize. Always remember this, reader—someone is always watching to see how you will come out of a situation, especially when they are going through the same thing. Your story is what keeps them hanging on. I have watched my sister bravely raise three children as a single mother, and I am sure that many days she wanted to give up. However, she didn't give up on her children, herself, or her God, and because of that, she is a reflection of a woman with an unbreakable spirit.

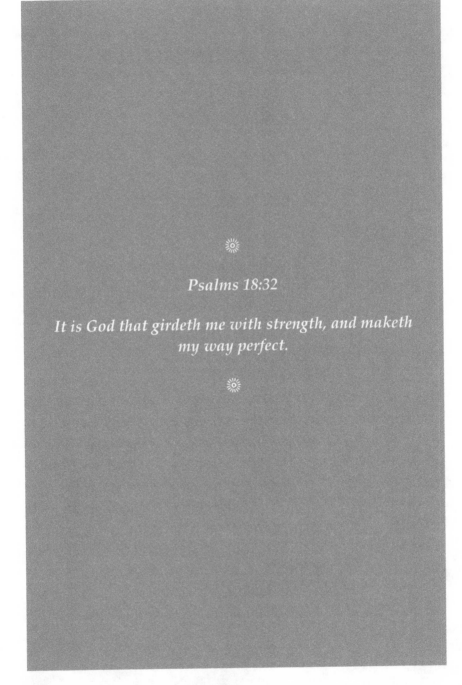

Psalms 18:32

It is God that girdeth me with strength, and maketh my way perfect.

" UNBREAKABLE"

A fraid and brave, but not broken
Beaten and battered but not broken
Black, held back but not broken

Hurt, healed and whole but not broken

Walked on, talked about, had plenty, been without but not broken

Cried all night, lied about, had to fight but not broken

been hired, been fired, but not broken

Scared and confused been abused but not broken

Cut down, built up, been down, been up but not broken

Banged up, chained up, threw up my hands when I have had enough but not broken

Dressed up, messed up, hair long, hair cut but not broken

No job, been robbed, but not broken

Been in pain, hung my head in shame but not broken

Been ignored, been restored, been busy, been bored but not broken

Stayed up, prayed up, black girl you were made to be tough

Throw your shoulders back and hold your head up

You are unbreakable and you are enough.

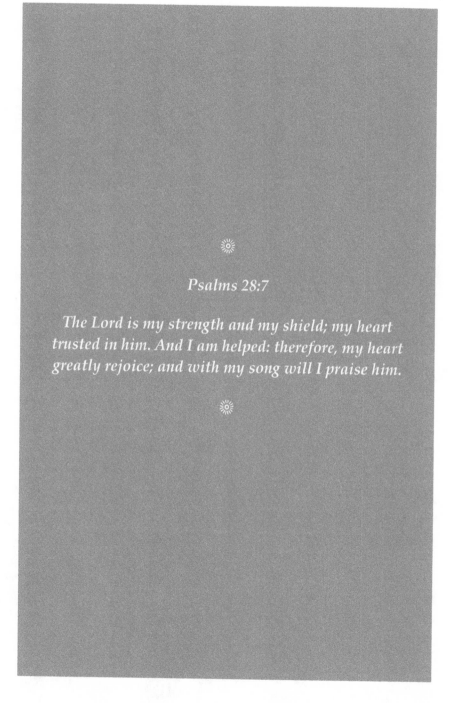

Psalms 28:7

The Lord is my strength and my shield; my heart trusted in him. And I am helped: therefore, my heart greatly rejoice; and with my song will I praise him.

"That Tree"

Dear Lord, when I think about the cross, I think of the sacrifice you made for me. No one else could have done this for me. I love you Lord. I am filled with gratitude because of salvation, the free gift of life. It seems as though the only time the world talks about the cross is during "easter". But to the church, that special day is Resurrection Sunday—the day you rose from the grave. The tree represents salvation. The Cross is something I think about every time I fall on my knees and spend time with you in prayer. My sins hung on that "Tree" for you and for me. If I had ten thousand tongues it wouldn't be enough to say thank you for what you have done. You are my whole life, Jesus.

I pray that as you read this poem, you would take a moment to reflect on the love that hung on the cross—yes, that tree.

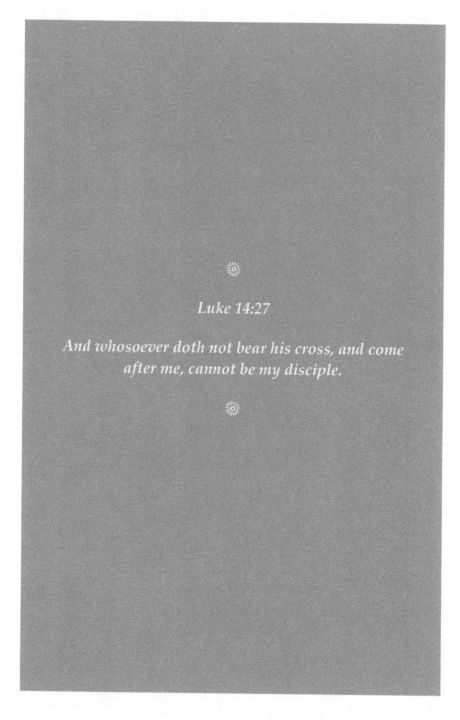

Luke 14:27

And whosoever doth not bear his cross, and come after me, cannot be my disciple.

Acts 5:30

The God of our Fathers raised up Jesus, whom ye slew, and hanged on a tree.

"THAT TREE"

When I think of you, I think of the tree,
When I fall to my knees

I look up to thee

That tree where my sins hung for me

It was you on the tree you did it so that I could be free

I see your love hanging on that tree

Your love took the place for me on the tree

Must Jesus bare the cross alone

And the whole world go free

There is a cross for you and there is a cross for me

I am not worthy, no not me

But your love hung on that old, rugged tree

You hung your head and you died for me

But you rose from the dead, on day three

I will never understand why you did it for me

I think about it every time I fall to my knees

What a sacrifice that was made for me

On that faithful day on Mt. Calvary

Jesus Christ set me free

Sin no longer has a hold on me

If you only knew what he did for me

When he took up the cross, yes that tree

And that is why I fall to my knees

And say thank you Lord, you did it for me on the cross

yes THAT TREE

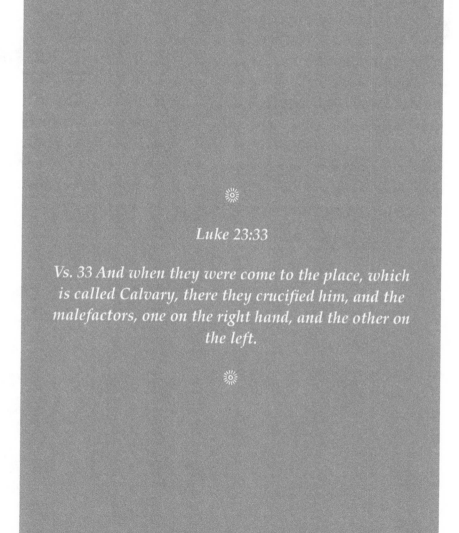

Luke 23:33

Vs. 33 And when they were come to the place, which is called Calvary, there they crucified him, and the malefactors, one on the right hand, and the other on the left.

In closing I would like to personally say thank you for your continued love, support, and prayers. Thank you for purchasing this book of Poetry and Inspirational writings I pray that it blessed you and maybe even opened your eyes to some hard truths about this thing we call life. I have experienced everything that I have written about, racial divide, rejection, pain, and self-confidence to name a few and out of all of that God produced Pearls. It sounds crazy for me to say this but praise God in the hard times and not only when things are going well, you will discover that is where he will meet you, in the hard times. When your vessel is empty, allow God to pour out his blessings in you, fill you with his Spirit, His word, and His Love, so that you may be able to pour into others.

God bless you all

Psalms 9:9-10

Vs. 9 The Lord also will be a refuge for the oppressed,
a refuge in times of troubles.

Vs. 10 And they that know thy name will put their
trust in thee: for thou, Lord, hast not forsaken them
that seek thee.

Reflection

**Spend time reflecting on these words and the promises
that God has for your life:
Isaiah 41:10**

_____

_____

_____

_____

_____

_____

_____

_____

_____

_____

_____

_____

_____

_____

_____

_____

_____

_____

_____

_____

_____

_____

_____

Reflection
Matthew 11:28

Acknowledgements

I would like to first thank my children—Tyree, Trey, and Sara for their patience with me as I spent countless hours writing and calling on them for their opinions and advice. Thank you for loving me as your mother and your prayer warrior, even when I would get on your nerves. I cannot forget my beautiful grandchildren. They complete me and I love them with every fiber of my being. They are truly a blessing to my soul. I cannot forget my one and only daughter-in-law. Thank you for supporting me in ways that no one else knew except you, me, and God. Although your mother is thousands of miles away, you call me mom, and that is special to me.

To my earthly dad, Richard Green, my siblings (my seven pillars of strength), and my one and only sister-in-love and four brother-in-laws, thank you very much for your continuous support through this book and the next ones to come. I love you all so deeply. God truly blessed me when he allowed me to be in this family that is knitted tightly together with love.

Thank you to Dr. Janell Jones of Melanin Grace Publishing Company. You have been a blessing to me while coaching me through this process. I remember when I first met you over 20 years ago. You had such a beautiful and jovial spirit. Look at how God has prospered and blessed you over the years. Thank you to my Bishop of 24 years at The Mt. Hermon Missionary Baptist Church for the preached word and spiritual guidance. I have to say thank you to a very special friend, neighbor, and spiritual leader, Roger Stowe. For 25 years you have been a friend to me, and I say this with tears in my eyes. I am not ashamed to tell the world how much I love you for never giving up on me and for never ceasing to pray for me. I have many people to say thank you to but there is a special lady, Chef Michelle Willoughby, who was my instructor in Culinary School. God has brought her back into my life through our job. Thank you, Chef, for your obedience to the Holy Spirit when I was going through some of my darkest days. God has blessed me with a large support group and if I have not called you by name in my acknowledgments, please charge it to my head and not my heart. All of you are special to me and you know what role you played in my life and in this endeavor. I pray that this book will mend broken relationships, heal hurts, restore joy, and bless the reader. God bless you all.

The Author

*S*hannon D. Morgan is the youngest of eight children born to Richard and Glenda Green. Shannon has dedicated her life to being a mother of three children, grandmother of nine amazing grandchildren, and one daughter-in-law.

After Shannon retired from The OSU Wexner Medical Center in 2006 as Administrative Assistant on the BMT Unit, she pursued her dream in the Culinary industry, by attending the Columbus Culinary Institute @ Bradford. Shannon graduated in the Spring of 2009 with an Associate's Degree in Culinary Arts and Design.

Immediately after receiving her degree in Culinary Arts, Shannon began working in the food industry as a Private Chef for various clients in Columbus, Ohio. She has also catered numerous weddings, graduation parties, and special events.

Shannon has worked under some of Ohio's finest chefs in various food industries throughout her culinary career, while continuing to grow, learn, and perfect her culinary knowledge and skills. However, Shannon could not ignore her inner voice calling her to help those in the homeless and lower income communities. In 2007, with the help of God, Shannon started a non-profit organization called C.H.E.F. (Cooking to Help Families). Through C.H.E.F., she provided free cooking demonstrations at community and recreation centers and food pantries to educate families on how to stretch their food dollars and shop the perimeters of grocery stores.

Shannon's C.H.E.F. program was featured on local news station, WBNS10tv in February 2012, on the Female Focus segment. In April of 2014, Shannon received a Volunteer of the Year Award from Eat'n Park Hospitality Group. In 2017 she received an Achievement Award while working for Aramark at Capital University. Shannon continues to serve in the food industry, currently at Columbus State Community College.

Shannon decided to step out on faith to share some of her writings in a book of poetry after writing for years as a hobby. Shannon is a devout woman of God and member of the Mt. Hermon Missionary Baptist Church where she has served for over twenty years. While Shannon serves the Lord, she continues to seek opportunities to serve her community as well.

Resources

The Prayer of Pearls is a free resource designed to give you help, encouragement, and strength. This is a prayer that you can use daily to increase your walk with God. http://bit.ly/ prayerofpearls

References:

King James Bible. (2020). King James Bible Online. https://www.kingjamesbibleonline.org

CPSIA information can be obtained
at www.ICGtesting.com
Printed in the USA
FSHW010743040521
80998FS